Dominate Procrastination - Tips, Hacks and Strategies to Stop Procrastinating and Skyrocket Your Productivity

By James Oliver

"Procrastination is like a credit card: it's a lot of fun until you get the bill." - Christopher Parker

Contents

Dominate Procrastination - Tips, Hacks and Strategies to Stop Procrastinating and Skyrocket Your Productivity
By James Oliver
Contents
Introduction - Why on Earth Did I Write This Book?
Procrastination Is Killing You
Procrastination Is Not Laziness
The Lizard Brain, Instant Gratification And Taking a Long Term View Of The Situation
You Are Going To Mess Up
Procrastination and Guilt
Your Brain Wants You to Fail
The Consumer vs. Producer Mentality
Avoiding Burnout - 5 Ways to Stay Productive in The Long Run
Your Guru Is Not Perfect
Deadlines - And Why Everything Takes Less Time Than You Think
Doing vs. Planning
The Importance of Making a Start
The Glory of Ignoring Email
The Rule of Three
The Eisenhower Principle and Urgent vs. Important Activities
The Pareto Principle and the 80/20 Rule
The Importance of a Morning Routine
Keeping a Time Log
Why You Should Never Multi-Task
Why Writers Block Is a Myth That Doesn't Exist
Physical Exercise and Productivity
The Pomodoro Technique and the (10+2)*5 Method
Why You Should Never Tell Anyone Your Goals
Making Your Life Easier for Yourself By Minimizing Decisions
Everyday Focus Tools
Why I Don't Recommend Chemical Enhancement for Productivity
Afterword - Intrinsic Motivation - Why We Do What We Do
Bibliography

Introduction - Why on Earth Did I Write This Book?

Hi,

I'm James - you won't have heard of me.

I'm just a regular guy doing regular guy things like writing for a living and trying not to waste away my life looking at pictures of beaches on Instagram.

In other words - I'm just like you.

For the majority of my life I was a chronic procrastinator. I used to spend 12 hours a day mindlessly browsing the internet, binge watching TV shows and chatting with friends on IM (RIP MSN Messenger).

What's worse though, is that I was always seeking out ways to remove this procrastination. I consumed productivity books, read countless articles on the internet and yet never bothered applying the information or techniques.

Then one day everything just clicked. I woke up knowing that if I didn't pull my finger out, I'd be stuck in the same dead-end corporate job for the next 40 years, dreaming of that inflation busting 3% pay rise or extra vacation day.

Once I figured out how to stop letting these destructive acts take over my life, I realized something - I could be productive and more importantly, I could achieve things.

I want to share with you some techniques and strategies that I personally employ to stay on top of my game and avoid the procrastination monster.

Procrastination Is Killing You

It's not literally killing you in the same vein as cigarettes or meth, but it is killing your art, your productivity and your ideas.

Every year billions of dollars and countless accolades are left unclaimed by missed opportunities, unfinished projects and ideas that never come to fruition.

I was browsing Reddit recently and stumbled upon a thread titled "What is the biggest example of wasted potential in human history"

This answer jumped out immediately - "We don't know, they probably weren't notable enough"

Bar a crippling physical or mental disability, everyone has the potential to achieve something great. Even with such a condition, you could still absolutely reach far beyond what you think is possible. No, not everyone will be Fortune 500 CEOs or NFL quarterbacks, but they can fulfill their own potential, create something of real value and reach the pinnacles of their own ability.

Nike has the single best slogan in the corporate world. Just Do It - those 3 words alone have generated billions of dollars worth of revenue for the sportswear giant. Why? Because it speaks to our yearning for greatness. Our inate desire to accomplish, achieve and make a difference.

However, taking action is a little trickier than just doing it. After all you wouldn't just tell an obese person to "just stop eating" - they'd need a little more encouragement and structure than that. What most of us need is a solid set of tactics and processes up our sleeves to overcome the nagging beast known as procrastination.

To do this we first have to examine why we procrastinate and the different types of procrastination. Then once we have an understanding of why we truly pursue these self-destructive habits, we can tackle them head on.

Procrastination Is Not Laziness

It's common to label procrastination and laziness in the same boat, and while there may be some overlap between the two, it's important to understand the different motivators that these things encompass.

The fundamental difference is this - Laziness is not wanting to do the work. Procrastination is a fear of the doing the work that matters.

Lazy people don't clean their rooms, procrastinators clean their rooms twice or three times a week. It's not that we don't want to work, it's that we're afraid of doing work that will move the needle. You see, many procrastinators have an acute fear of success, a fear of being able to accomplish something.

Success requires us to the do the uncomfortable, the unfamiliar and the unexpected. It requires us to approach tasks from different mindsets than we're used to, and involves acknowledging that we're probably going to make mistakes along the way. No one became successful by living in comfort and not pushing their boundaries, in fact the most successful people on Earth are the ones who are constantly avoiding this comfort zone.

We also associate success with being in a position of scrutiny, and criticism. In the artistic world, the term "selling out" has become commonplace, the idea that if your work has monetary value, it now somehow has less artistic value.

This doesn't just apply to our work, we fear that we may change who we are at the core. We should think of this not in a negative light (will I lose who I am?), but in a positive one (what additions will I make?).

Embracing the process is an important mindset in overcoming these psychological barriers. On the surface we may only have our end goal in mind, but unless we are willing to embrace what it takes to get there, you're unlikely to reach your final destination. Taking stock of a situation, looking at a task and saying out loud "this might suck, but it's necessary" are vital parts of the equation. Resilience and grit are more important in the path to success than any college degree, "creative gene" or technical skillset.

We approach this idea in greater detail later on in perfection vs. progress.

The Lizard Brain, Instant Gratification And Taking a Long Term View Of The Situation

Our Amygdala, or lizard brain, is the oldest part of the brain stem. The part that controls our fight or flight instincts and our emotions without the need to process additional information. Now that we've evolved past food, shelter and sex - and more importantly, past the potential for death at every corner, this lizard brain seeks gratification in other forms. In Steven Pressfield's book D*o The Work*[i] - he talks about this part of the brain in terms of resistance.

"Resistance is an active, intelligent, protean, malign, force — tireless, relentless and inextinguishable — whose sole object is to stop us from becoming our best selves and from achieving our higher goals."

In terms of our goals - resistance is procrastination, and procrastination is resistance.

Procrastination satisfies our lizard brain, the "ugh yeah" reflex that we all possess. The rawest form of ourselves, the caveman gene if you will. The need for instant gratification, short term happiness and more importantly our need for survival. Those YouTube videos that make us laugh, those Facebook posts that make us angry or that video game that just takes us away from the real world for an hour or two.

Our lizard brain also makes us terrible at weighing up costs and benefits through different time periods. We favor and prioritize short, small rewards over long, larger ones.

Unfortunately, beyond a lobotomy, the lizard brain is here for the long haul. We just need to figure out a way to quieten its instincts. To do this we need to focus on taking a long term view of a situation, being able to do this is key to overcoming our self-resistance. Being able to see how what you accomplish today is going to help you achieve your ultimate goal in the future. Delayed gratification is the biggest tool in your arsenal in the war against procrastination. The sooner your realize and embrace this, the quicker you can be on your path to personal greatness.

You may be familiar with the famous Stanford Marshmallow Experiment. Conducted in the 1960s, Professor Walter Mischel carried out various delayed gratification studies on young children. The experiment involved sitting the children down individually in a room and offering them one of two choices. They could eat a single marshmallow there and then, or they could wait 15 minutes and be rewarded with two marshmallows.

The result were quite frankly astounding, after follow up studies were done throughout the children's adolescence, the children who chose to wait for the second marshmallow recorded higher SAT scores, lower levels of substance abuse and lower obesity rates. In fact, these experiments continued for over 40 years and those who favored delayed gratification outperformed the short term satisfaction subjects in EVERY. CONCEIVABLE. MEASURE.

Whilst a single University study is not the be all end all of success, it does demonstrate one vital thing. If you want to achieve something great, at some point you will have to take the harder path. You will have sacrifice something in the short term to move towards your long term goal.

to five years in one career field, and be totally dedicated to the process – including being committed to the work of studying and working with the best. You must put into action what you have learned in this book to realize not only your full potential, but also your ability to reach your goals. With what you know now, you have the responsibility to become a mighty Job Magnet!

I pray that this book has been helpful to you on your employment journey, and that it will help you develop your career in an expansive and totally fulfilling way. If you desire more assistance, you can contact me for coaching or training by visiting my web site at www.howtogetajobin90days.net or www.therelationshipengineer.com.

You Are Going To Mess Up

One of the most common traits of procrastinators is an acute fear of failure on their path to success. You see success and failure go hand in hand. In our path to success we have a fear that we will somehow be humiliated in our pursuit of greatness. This fear paralyzes us into inaction. After all, it's pretty hard to fail at spending all day on Facebook as opposed to working on your novel.

When tattoo artist and Inkmaster star Shane O'Neill was asked if he ever messes up a tattoo, he famously responded "Of course I do." When one of the best tattoo artists on the planet can admit he makes mistakes that are imprinted on people's bodies for life, you know he's reached the pinnacle of his profession.

The first time you do anything, it's going to be bad. The first time you try to ride a bike, the first time you try to swim, and the first time you try to execute a business idea. Walt Disney was fired from his job at the Kansas City Star newspaper because his editor believed he "lacked ideas and imagination". Facebook was originally conceived as a variation of the popular hotornot.com for Harvard students. Let's just say that the idea wasn't particularly well received. I think Mark Zuckerberg did OK after that though…

What Zuckerberg and these other titans of their craft understand is how to adapt and evolve, and learn from their mistakes and failures. The old cliche "you will learn more from your mistakes, than your successes" could not be more appropriate in this respect.

The true professional is never satisfied in their work, they are always looking for ways to be better, they know that consistent progress is the way to greatness. Not perfection, but progress. Progress is something you can achieve every single day of your life, perfection is an unattainable pursuit that only leads to unhappiness.

Mistakes force us to learn, they force us to adapt. Mistakes allow us to open up to new perspectives and theories. Being able to accept your own mistake increased your enthusiasm and drive to progress towards your goals.

Perfectionism is a loyal friend of the procrastinator. It's an easy way out of doing a task. The thought that we need to do everything perfectly the first time, and every subsequent time after that. You are going to have bad days, but what is important is how we get back on the horse after these. Maybe you had a day where everything at work went wrong and your motivation was sapped, leaving you unwilling to do anything else but sit on the couch and watch Netflix. That's okay. You can have days like this, as long as they are an exception and not the rule. It's important to remember that not everybody is "on" all the time, but likewise you must strive to progress in your life and ensure your Netflix slob days are a rarity.

Procrastination and Guilt

These two devils of the mind go hand in hand. A study in 2000[ii] showed that guilt is one of the few emotions that we actually experience <u>at the time</u> of procrastinating. While we may be avoiding an unpleasant task and indulging in an unproductive one, which is rewarding and perhaps pleasant - a nagging feeling of guilt often undermines the good feelings that task avoidance may bring. That deep seated knowledge of what you should be doing vs. what you are doing. This ties in with the instant gratification explanation that we enjoy the short terms benefits but are aware of the long-term costs of continued procrastination. This guilt has a snowball effect of putting us in a worse mood by lowering our emotional and cognitive energy - two things we absolutely need to accomplish productive tasks.

Experiencing guilt while putting off a task is a surefire signal that this task is worth doing. Listen to your emotions the next time you find yourself distracted by the internet when you should be doing something productive to move closer to your goals.

Your Brain Wants You to Fail

As long as humans are alive on this Earth, we will engage in the practice of self-sabotage. Instead of reaching our full potential, we can make excuses as to why we didn't. The luck that didn't go our way, the delayed train that made us late for our date, the market downturn that meant our business idea didn't pan out.

Self-sabotage protects our self-esteem during the undertaking of difficult tasks. If we simply put off something that appears tough, it can't defeat us. Believing you can't do something is the easiest way to avoid doing it. The long-term effect however is a lingering feeling of lack of fulfilment. That knowledge that we could have indeed tried harder and achieved more.

However, changing your mindset to believing you can tackle these challenges and overcome them puts you in a position to confront task's head on rather than pushing them to the side, and eventually avoiding them all together.

The incremental mindset allows us to take small steps in a positive direction. Asking yourself "is what I accomplished today going to benefit me tomorrow?" is a great way to do this. Judge yourself not by the outcome, but by the effort. Remember to start small with any task.

The Consumer vs. Producer

Mentality

There are two types of people in this world. Those who are majority consumers, and those who are majority producers. Producers are ones whose net worth is constantly on the increase; consumers are the ones whose net worth never breaks past a certain level. Producers are the ones who create art, businesses, and wealth while consumers create ideas that never come to fruition.

Tom Cruise is a producer, he makes movies, and he gets paid fairly handsomely for the privilege. Everyone who goes to the theatre to watch his movie is a consumer. Is this type of consumption bad? Not necessarily, in moderation. However, with chronic procrastinators it is consumption in excess that we are concerned with.

Back in my teenage years I set myself the arbitrary goal of trying to watch all the movies on the IMDB Top 250 movie list. I wasn't an aspiring film student, in fact at that time people would probably have described me as the least creative person ever, but I wanted to watch all these movies to get a sense of accomplishment. This is a prime example of excess consumption in action. We as a society have been moving in this direction for some time now. Terms like "binge watching" are part of our lexicon and we glorify spending an entire weekend with our best friend Netflix. Not only is this harmful to our physical health (as anything with the word binge tends to be), it's harmful to our mentality.

The other part of this problem is spending our time doing the work for someone else, without even realizing it. Take a site like reddit.com, a multi-million dollar website, and yet its owners have to spend $0 producing content every year, because it's all user generated. Some of the best information on certain subjects is on reddit, and yet the users who produced it aren't getting compensated for their time. There are even cases now of reddit content being "re-purposed" (read: stolen) by other websites, so now two different people are making money from these posts, neither of which is the person who wrote them in the first place!

Now how do we approach this from a personal standpoint? We simply ask ourselves the question of "Am I producing or consuming right now?" This doesn't mean we all have to go out an attempt to remake Mission Impossible (although I support this as a goal), but we can align our day-to-day endeavors with a larger purpose. In more practical terms, instead of writing a forum post for someone else, post your thoughts and ideas on a personal blog.

This is especially valuable with how we start our day. Think back to our lizard brains. If we begin our day consuming as much information as you can, and with cell phones and social media that's never been easier, then we are likely to continue this habit throughout the rest of the day. If we begin the day as a producer, our lizard brains are quietened and less likely to reappear even later in the day. If you're a writer, the best time to write is as soon as you wake up, even before you've had breakfast. There are countless examples of famous writers getting all their work done before noon. Kurt Vonnegut and Haruki Murakami are just two examples of legendary writers who liked to get all their work done before midday.

Avoiding Burnout - 5 Ways to Stay Productive in The Long Run

One of the more common problems people have on their journey to be productive is once they decide to make a change in their lives, they over exert themselves too fast and as a result, crash and burn which leaves them reverting back to their previous bad habits.

Anyone who has been a member of a gym for a long time understands the January rush. All the people who swore they would "get in shape" as a New Year's Resolution suddenly descend on the YMCAs and the Planet Fitnesses of the world. These temporarily inspired souls go balls to the wall, hitting the gym 5 or 6 days a week…for about a month, before reverting back to their prior ways.

No one is productive all the time. Anyone who says they are is a liar, or a modafinil addict. We are human beings, not single task focused productivity robots. Pushing yourself too far inevitably leads to burnout, which only results in more pain and suffering and a tendency to lean the other way and procrastinate harder than ever before. Try taking these steps to avoid burnout and maintain productivity over a longer period of time.

1. Create a reward system: Take one act of consumption that you really enjoy, be it watching a movie or posting hilarious memes on Facebook. Instead of beginning your day with that act, use it as a reward for yourself *AFTER* you accomplish the tasks at hand (remember delayed gratification). Implementing a system like this has two benefits. Number one, it allows our brains to satisfy our consumption needs, which keeps us from avoiding burnout and two, it incentivizes us to finish the task itself. If you want, add your reward to your to-do list, but ensure that you only indulge yourself after your work is complete.

2. Have a third space: Your third space is somewhere you go that isn't your workplace or your home (if you work from home then this would technically be a second space). This should be somewhere you can visit frequently and feel at ease, like a coffee shop or a bar. It's also an advantage if you space is a place of community gathering, where you know other people by name and can sit down and have a conversation. Your third space should also be highly accessible, ideally within walking distance but a short drive or train ride is OK -

you don't want to have built in excuses as to why you can't visit somewhere. This space will allow you to mentally unwind in a setting that has a level of comfort and familiarity.

3. Maintain social connections. This is one that I still struggle with. You're so invested in whatever project you're working on that you sometimes shun social events to focus on work, with the perceived notion that spending time with others makes you lazy or unproductive. Remember, people love you regardless of your productivity levels so it's important to keep them in your life. The best way to stay on top of this is to schedule regular social activities, joining a sports team is the perfect solution here and has the added benefit of providing essential physical exercise to keep our endorphin levels up.

4. Only compare yourself to yourself. In the internet age we're exposed to the lives of billions of people, and we've never seen so many "successful" ones in history. The entrepreneurs posting their private jets on social media, the "mastermind" groups on Facebook where people share screenshots of their 6-figure passive income businesses. All this does is force us to compare ourselves to these outwardly successful people. We have to remember that a) These people have their own internal struggles which they rarely share on these mediums and b) It doesn't matter what anyone else is doing. You should only compare your results to yourself. You've *only* written half a book? Well that's half a book more than you'd written last year. You've *only* lost 10lbs, well you're now 10lbs closer to your goal. By

using ourselves as the yardstick, it's much easier for us to monitor progress and be in a frame of mind where we seek continued advances.

5. Get enough sleep. We've all seen the stories of politicians and CEOs who sleep 4 hours a night, and good for them. Hollywood movies regular glamorizes the "pulling an all nighter" scene in fields such as education, law and investment banking. However, us mere mortals require a minimum of 6 hours sleep, and most of us function drastically better on 8. In fact, a study by the non-profit RAND organisation[iii] found that lack of sleep costs the US economy around $400 billion dollars each year through lost work days. Even as far back as 1880, studies demonstrated that our returns diminished when working more than 40 hours a week as we spent more time rectifying mistakes made due to fatigue. Without even accounting for the physical benefits of more sleep, let's examine the productivity centric ones.

Sleeping helps improve your decision making, and being able to prioritize certain tasks. We're also better at re-focusing on a task at hand when we're well rested. No more 5-minute breaks that turn into 2-hour Wikipedia deep dives. Sleep also leads to an overall improvement in our mood, which is essential if we want to get anything done. When we're deprived, our parietal and occipital lobes (which are responsible for processing sensory data) lose glucose, making it harder to concentrate and make accurate judgments about the world around us.

A word on naps, while I am not a fan of them personally, they can be useful to many people. Taking a quick 5- to 15-minute rest when you realize you are procrastinating or just in a productivity lull will leave you waking up refreshed and ready to get back on task. There is some evidence that drinking caffeine 15-20 minutes before a nap can leave you waking even more refreshed than just napping or consuming the caffeine as isolated events. So, if you're stuck for some new productivity ideas, try a coffee nap for size and see how you react.

Your Guru Is Not Perfect

No one is perfect - and that's OK.

The problem with certain gurus, or successful people in the public eye is that they glorify certain aspects of their life. Sleeping for less than 5 hours, waking up at 4AM and working 16 hours days while training for marathons are just some examples of this.

The fact of the matter is this, for 99.9% of people this is completely unsustainable. Most people don't want to go through life feeling like a zombie. What's more is that many of these people do this routine for show. I can categorically say that there are a minute amount of people who function well on less than 6 hours sleep a night. What's more is that there are a far bigger percentage who manage to get all their shit done within 8 hours of work a day.

The truth of the matter is you don't have to be a superhuman to achieve something great. You just have to prioritize correctly. Remember, for every Spiderman there is a Peter Parker inside.

Deadlines - And Why Everything

Takes Less Time Than You Think

Deadlines, whether self-imposed or set by your customers or partners, force us to get things done. However, they're also a fantastic cause of wasted time. This is because we as a society overestimate the time needed to complete specific tasks, and as such, waste an inordinate amount of it knowing that we don't *really* have to accomplish anything in the next hour/today/this week, as our deadline is still a long way off.

The first time this came to light for me was in my final year of studying Economics at University. I had an assignment due the following morning. I'd spent the best part of 3 weeks working on it, and by working on it I mean spending an hour on the project itself followed by 2 playing video games and 3 more watching TV.

The night before it was due, I miraculously managed to delete the entire thing when transferring it from my laptop to the school's remote server. To this day I don't know how I did it*. I was in a panic; how could I possibly re-do the entire thing in less than 24 hours? Well the fact was that I didn't really have a choice, I just had to. 4 hours and a few cups of a coffee later, I'd re-written the entire thing from memory. When I had a hard time constraint, I was forced to take massive action, and this was the result. The assignment got an A by the way.

Those nagging tasks that you don't really want to do, that message you should really respond to, the job application you should submit. In our heads we build these up as monumental hurdles, when they are in fact the smallest of them. The amount of times I've mentally prepared an hour to respond to email when in reality it takes about 7 minutes is astounding.

For those of you in the corporate world. Stop scheduling meetings to be an hour long. Most of this hour is spent chitchatting and nothing gets accomplished. If the meetings were now 13 minutes long instead, I guarantee every single one of those minutes would be productive. Try setting yourself increasingly short periods of time to get things done. Author and Motivational Coach Stefan James famously set himself a goal to write a book in 24 hours. He achieved just that, and even wrote a book on that exact subject. I'm not saying you have to go to these extremes right off the bat, but once you get in the habit of doing it, you'll question why you didn't start sooner.

British historian Cyril Parkinson expanded on this with a view to the corporate world, with what came to be known as Parkinson's Law - "Work expands so as to fill the time available for its completion"

Parkinson realized that, despite having less and less paperwork in the British Colonial Office, the number of employees increased each year by more than 5%. By setting tighter deadlines for yourself, you limit yourself to only focusing on what is truly important to your end goal.

Psychology and Behavioral Economics professor Dan Ariely[iv] (whose book *Predictably Irrational* should be a must read for anyone with an interest in human behavior) once did an experiment where he hired a group of 60 people to proofread three passages. One group got a weekly deadline for each passage, a second group got one deadline at the end of the month for all three passages, and the third group chose their own deadlines. Readers were rewarded for the errors they found and penalized $1 for each day they were late. Group II performed the worst. The group that with the regular weekly (shortest) deadlines performed the best.

*Author's note: Keep multiple backups of everything important, preferably both physical and digital

Doing vs. Planning

Planning and procrastination go hand-in-hand. How many times do we see college kids spend days making a study schedule rather than just studying?

Over planning is a direct substitute for doing. Procrastinators love to make grandiose yet vague plans that don't account for any action being taken.

Making a plan fuels our need for instant gratification and sense of accomplishment, despite the plan not having accomplished anything.

Effective planning focuses on one singular goal. Whether that be to make your first $1 from a business idea or to ace your next exam, make sure all your plans focus on that goal.

This goes as far as starting a business. A study by Bentley University[v] found that 66% of millennials have a desire to start their own business, 37% would like to work for themselves, and 25% would like to own their own company. Yet, as of 2013, only 3.6% of all businesses were owned by someone under the age of 30. The desire/follow through ratio is 20:1 - and you can guess where most of these people didn't follow through - the planning stage.

No one "builds a business." They perform one task at a time and the end result is a business. Procrastinators are great visionaries—they love to fantasize about the end result, the great product or service they've built and the money they've made. What they need to do is focus on the tasks that will get them to that end result. The design, the testing, the customer research.

Almost all big projects can be broken down into single units of progress. Bodybuilders don't just think about getting in incredible shape, they go to the gym day after day and accomplish single sessions designed to get them to their goal physique.

Dancers don't just think about learning a routine, they practice each individual step over and over again until they are tied together into a spectacular performance.

The Importance of Making a Start

If you perpetually put something off because you feel unsure of how to do it, just start. You may do a shitty job at first, but 1) you will have proven to yourself you can do it in some form, and 2) you'll be able to learn from your mistakes.

Let's look at momentum in a different way. One of the most terrifying things as a new author is the idea that no one will buy your book. Especially in the age where publishing a book has never been easier or cheaper. You put the book up on Amazon and you see that overarching reaper-like statistic of 0 reviews. But when that zero turns into a 1, a huge sigh of relief washes over you. Because if 1 person bought your book and liked it, why not 2? why not 10? why not 100?

The Zeigarnik effect is a wonderful phenomenon that can be boiled down to one sentence. When common people start something, they tend to finish it. It's much easier to avoid starting something than it is to to fall away from a task that you're already in the process of doing. We can compound this to our advantage by starting with the easier part of the project. Instead of worrying about the difficult part, approach the easiest part first. This creates momentum, and momentum is invaluable in assisting you in accomplishing projects.

The Glory of Ignoring Email

Email may well be the biggest enemy of the procrastinator today. Not social media, but email. We feel less guilty spending time on our email accounts than we do on Facebook or Twitter. Email has this odd "I'm being productive, I promise" feel to it. Email is a wonderful method of mass communication, but a horrible method of 1-to-1 communication. Nowadays, instead of sorting out a problem over the phone (or God forbid, face to face) in 5 minutes, we spend an hour emailing back and forth before anything gets done.

I suggest limiting your email use to 2 periods of 10 minutes per day, neither of these being first thing in the morning. I usually use 12PM and 5PM just because that's when my schedule affords me a break. You'll find that when you do this, something magical happens - you get way more done before, and the people sending you emails don't even notice your non-immediate response.

But what about emergencies? Well 1. They don't really exist in the world of email and 2. You can write in your email signature that you would prefer phone communication in the rare case of an actual emergency.

The Rule of Three

"Make a to-do list" is one of the most common answers to people's search to end procrastination. People get all excited and before they know it, they've written down 10, 20 or even 50 things that they "need" to finish. This ever-growing list becomes exhausting to even look at, and as a result never gets done. You see people love to fill their lists with low priority tasks like making the bed (this should be something you do every day, it doesn't warrant a special place) and concentrate on those - by the time they've even thought about approaching their actual work, it's too late and they're off watching cat videos again.

That's why I'm suggesting you limit your to-do list to three tasks every day. These three tasks will directly advance you on your path to your goal. By limiting your list to only three tasks, you are much more likely to finish every one of these three on a consistent basis.

The Eisenhower Principle and Urgent vs. Important Activities

President Eisenhower once said in a 1954 speech "I have two kinds of problems: the urgent and the important. The urgent are not important, and the important are never urgent."

He used this guiding principle to prioritize his tasks for the day.

Important activities have an outcome that leads to us achieving our goals, whether these are professional or personal.

Urgent activities demand immediate attention, and are usually associated with achieving someone else's goals. They are often the ones we concentrate on and they demand attention because the consequences of not dealing with them are immediate.

By being able to utilize our time effectively, we spend more time on important problems than we do on urgent ones. If we don't tackle the important problems first, they often slip into the urgent category. For example, if you delay starting that essay until the night before it's due, the problem is now urgent rather than important.

The way we approach both problems is different as well. Important problems are attacked from an offensive position, we want to dominate and conquer them to the best of our abilities. Urgent problems are approached from a defensive position, we want to minimize the damage as much as possible and frankly just get the task over with. The latter more often than not results in lower quality work.

The Pareto Principle and the 80/20 Rule

While you may be aware of the Pareto principle, that 80% of the results come from 20% of the actions one takes, many of us still don't practice it.

How often do we hear of co-workers who are "swamped" or "having the busiest day", yet they manage to accomplish nothing over the course of 8 hours. Maybe this is you. The problem is working on activities of low-priority.

Even if you have a to-do list of just 3 items, it's likely that just one of those will be by far and away more important than the rest. This task is also likely to be the hardest one to complete.

Let's take an example of a freelance writer, they have a steady list of clients who pay them an OK, but not outstanding hourly rate. Instead of looking at ways to get more of these clients, examine a way to get a single client who pays you 3x your regular amount. This question is uncomfortable to tackle, and you will make excuses as to why you can't do it, but if you force yourself to, you will find a way. And as a result, you now have a significant income increase, without a significant increase in workload.

The Importance of a Morning Routine

The morning routine has long been a tool of the successful person. These people start their day with a purpose and an intent that unsuccessful people don't. I've long been fascinated with the routines of the rich and powerful. A solid morning routine puts in the right frame of mind to work without distractions.

Thanks to websites like http://mymorningroutine.com there's a huge database of routines from business leaders, TV personalities and entrepreneurs. After browsing hundreds of these, I've selected the key components that appear the most in these routines:

- Get out of bed as soon as you wake up
- Meditation
- Gratitude towards the self and others
- Thankfulness
- Physical exercise
- Drinking water
- Going outside
- Making a focused to-do list for the day

And perhaps unsuspectingly none of the routines featured the following:
- Check email
- Go on social media
- Watch TV
- Hit the snooze button

There is no perfect routine, and in fact I encourage you to try different routines and see what works for you.

Now directly after completing your morning routine, get right to work. Your brain is primed at this point in the day, you haven't been distracted by bad news, additional problems or the latest 20% off sale at your favourite clothing store. This is when your mind is at its clearest and when those "moments of inspiration" will come easiest to you.

Keeping a Time Log

There's a wonderful scene in The Office where Dwight Schrute claims that he works every single second of his 8-hour day. His colleague Jim Halpert challenges this claim by keeping a time log on all Dwight's activities, including bathroom breaks, breathing and drinking water. The point is this is to show that no one can be productive all the time, but on the flip-side it's a useful tool in determining just how much time we spend each day being unproductive.

Try it out, just for one day. Note down where all your time goes. How much time do you spend on the internet browsing social media? How much TV are you watching? It's guaranteed to be an enlightening process that will shock you into using your time better.

Why You Should Never Multi-Task

In our "not enough time in the day" society, multi-tasking has become commonplace everywhere from the office to the kitchen. Whether it's checking our email when we're in the bathroom, cooking dinner while trying to text someone back or trying to get three things done at once at our workplace - we're serial multi-taskers.

Multi-tasking is the act of accomplishing two or more tasks is a progressively less efficient manner. Your brain attempts valiantly to switch back and forth between them, but it just doesn't work. The thought of one task distracts you from the other, and thus you produce lower quality work. The facts are simple, you can do multiple tasks poorly, or you can do one task well. Research by the American Psychological Association[vi] has shown that multi-tasking reduces our productivity by up to 40%.

There's also a physical reaction to this, multi-tasking increases your heart rate and releases cortisol, the stress hormone which leads to us feeling overwhelmed.

This doesn't just apply to work related tasks. You should also make a conscious effort to apply this in your personal life. When your significant other is talking to you, put down your phone. When you're eating dinner, don't watch TV. By focusing on one thing at a time, you get a more enriching experience. You'll suddenly notice little things like your food tasting better all the way to connecting with your partner on a deeper level.

Why Writers Block Is a Myth That

Doesn't Exist

Writer's block is a 20th century invention. The term didn't even exist in a widespread manner until 1921. Before that writers just wrote. Seth Godin makes a fantastic point in his book "The Icarus Deception[vii]" that nobody ever suffers from "talker's block". Talking is a unedited, stream of consciousness action that allows us to express everything and anything that is on our mind.

Writing is the same thing, if you force yourself to sit down and write then you are going to accomplish a lot more than by sitting around for days, months or even years waiting for inspiration. Believe me 50,000 words is a lot more achievable when you sit down and force yourself to write 2,000 or even 200 of them a day.

I encourage you to try stream of consciousness writing, set yourself a target number of words or minutes and just go all out. Sit down and just type anything that comes to mind. Don't go back and edit, don't even check for typos - just write. Editing is a separate phase that can come at a later date.

There's a wonderful quote from writer William Faulkner when asked if he wrote every day or waited for inspiration before he put pen to paper. Faulkner responded with "I write when I'm inspired, and I see to it that I'm inspired at nine o'clock every morning."

One of my favourite examples of this is from legendary copywriter Gary Halbert, who happened to be a huge fan of this technique. In a draft of an ad for a new golf putter, he didn't know what the exact material used for the putter's handle grip was. Instead of stopping his work to find out (this was in the pre-internet age so would have required multiple phone calls), he simply wrote that the putter's grip was made from "the softest seal foreskin" before editing it at a later date when we had the information to hand.

Physical Exercise and Productivity

Exercise is great for both our physical and mental well-being. I can safely say all the times in life where I've had a prolonged period of depression or even feeling down were periods where I wasn't doing regular exercise. The 2PM slump that many of us suffer from, suddenly disappears when we work out regularly.

Exercise helps us stay alert and focused for a longer period of time. From a scientific standpoint, physical exertion enhances our bodies ability to transfer oxygen to the brain. In a University of Georgia randomized controlled trial, researchers split people into three groups – low-intensity, moderate-intensity and a control group (no exercise). During the six-week experiment, both exercise groups reported growing levels of energy compared to the control group.

It's also a great way to become "unstuck" in our work. If there's a certain task or problem that you can't seem to solve, go outside and take a walk for 10 or 15 minutes, this refreshes our brain's creative nodes.

The Pomodoro Technique and the (10+2)*5 Method

The Pomodoro technique is one of the most useful tools in the productive human's arsenal. Brought to popularity in the early 90s by Italian entrepreneur Francisco Cirillo, as a throwback to his days as an engineering student. There's nothing revolutionary about it really, it's simply working for 25 minutes, followed by 5 minutes of rest. Every 4 slots of 25 minutes, you take a longer break (I recommend at least 20 minutes).

By breaking up sessions like this, our brain can take a momentary break and reset. This refuels the creativity nodes and allows us to produce more good work for a longer period of time. By working in a series of short sprints, as opposed to a marathon, it is much easier to accomplish tasks. Once again, we come back to the central point of breaking up larger tasks into smaller, more manageable ones.

You'd be surprised by just how much work you can accomplish in only 25 minutes. You see the effect is twofold, not only do you now have less time to worry and stress about a situation, you also have a constraint on what you need to get done. This mental trick makes your brain believe that you must get as much done possible in these 25 minutes, lest the dreaded timer go off.

You can adapt this even further with the (10+2)*5 method. This strategy involves 10 minutes of work, followed by 2 minutes of rest, repeated 5 times. This gives you the same amount of total working time per hour (50 minutes) as the pomodoro method, but broken up into smaller chunks. The reasoning behind the shorter time periods is that your brain will enjoy the challenge of both the limited work and break periods of time and eventually look forward to both periods.

Why You Should Never Tell Anyone

Your Goals

One of the best TED talks I've ever seen is by CD Baby Founder Derek Sivers. It is simply titled "Keep Your Goals to Yourself"[viii]

A common problem people have with goal setting is the classic advice of telling everyone their goals. This is wrongly thought to bring a sense of accountability. A feeling that we will have let people down in we don't follow through with our intentions. Whilst this may indeed be the case for a certain group of people, it certainly isn't for the procrastinators among us.

This approach has the opposite effect. By telling people our goals, be it losing 15lbs or starting a business, we get a false sense of accomplishment. After all we've taken the step of "committing" to something, why wouldn't we? This temporary boost in self-esteem rarely lasts past a few days, and when it comes to actually taking time to work on the what we've promised to do, we falter and end up giving up on the project either before we started or before we've made any real progress.

The second part of this is that many of your closest friends DON'T want you to succeed. They don't want to see someone outperform their own lazy lifestyles and inability to make continued progress. This will cause them to consciously or subconsciously engage in behaviours that prevent you from achieving your highest desires.

Next time you have a big end goal in mind, don't tell anyone, not a soul. Instead simply write down what you want to accomplish in a personal diary and next to it write the steps you are going to take TODAY to move closer to said goal.

Making Your Life Easier for Yourself

By Minimizing Decisions

Too many decisions lead to too many indecisions. There is a lot to be said for repetition in certain areas of your life. Steve Jobs famously remarked that he wore the same outfit every day, not to be a style icon, but because it was one less decision for him to make every morning. This freed his brain up to make decisions for important things, like say, the launch of the iPod.

Picture your day tomorrow. What does it look like? Do you start the day with a feeling of calm and a sense of relaxation, or it is akin to waking up on a mental battlefield with chaos strewn everywhere? Even the tiniest steps like preparing a breakfast ahead of time or setting out what clothes you are going to where, can have a big impact the following day.

Everyday Focus Tools

There are a number of inexpensive tools both physical and digital that you can use to maintain productivity over a longer period of time.

Ear plugs

Probably not the revolutionary device you were expecting, but a $1 pair of ear plugs can certainly enhance your productivity. By blocking out external noise, your brain can channel in on what needs to be accomplished. This allows you to concentrate for longer periods of time and works especially well in conjunction with the pomodoro technique. You don't need to spend big to get a decent pair; you can easily pick ones up online costing just $5 for a set of 10.

Frequency radio stations on YouTube

I've never been a big fan of listening to music, podcasts or audiobooks while working. The latter two especially drag your brain focus away from the task at hand by providing something else to focus on. Instead what I recommend is frequency radio channels on YouTube. These channels provide ambient noise at specific frequency waves designed to enhance focus and productivity. If you are going to listen to music, instrumental mixes are preferable to vocal ones.

Noisli app - nature sounds and ambient noise - can choose different frequencies for productivity or relaxation, also has a built-in timer so it's great for those employing the pomodoro technique.
http://www.marinaratimer.com - Another pomodoro technique timer website

Useful web tools to prevent wasted computer hours

News Feed Eradicator for Facebook - Chrome Extension - Free - removes your newsfeed from Facebook, particularly useful if you need to use messenger to communicate or grab some photos but don't want to be distracted by everything else that Facebook has going on at a particular time.

StayFocusD - Chrome extension - free - allows you to block sites completely or limit your time spent on them each day. I personally recommend setting 5-minute limits for social media and 15-minute limits for your email

Why I Don't Recommend Chemical Enhancement for Productivity

Beyond caffeine, there are no drugs that are beneficial to *long term* productivity. Many gurus often champion different pills and substances of varying legal status. Everything from nootropics (aka "smart drugs) like piracetam or phenibut to controlled drugs like adderall and modafinil are used to give you an extra boost in the classroom or for personal projects.

The rise in nootropic supplements in particular has been staggering in these past 5 years as people looking for that competitive edge on the outside world. Once again, the glamorized position of using modafinil to stay up for 2 days straight has given these substances a certain credibility in the productivity field. There are even instances now of people livestreaming their all nighters on social media as part of a continued productivity war of sorts.

However, even ignoring the fact that many of these drugs are illegal to obtain without a prescription, there are so many downsides to this approach. Modafinil and adderall both enhance your brain's dopamine release. Dopamine is our reward neurotransmitter, the one that makes us happy. Too much happiness can't be a bad thing, surely?

Well if that happiness is now sourced from a chemical you're ingesting on a daily basis, your brain becomes desensitized to natural sources. In other words, by consuming these chemicals frequently we limit our natural happiness production. This is similar to how the comedown effect of MDMA and cocaine functions.

Your body always fights back. As with any chemical you input into your body, there is always an equal reaction once the chemical leaves your body. The same way smokers crave nicotine once that initial high is gone. Our body processes cognitive enhancement substances the same way, and long-term use can have undesirable negative effects. From anxiety and depression from withdrawal in the case of adderall, to an increased frequency of migraines (even if you have no prior history) with modafinil.

The other key factor in my reasoning is that there simply aren't enough controlled studies on the effectiveness of these pills. You're much better off getting a good night's sleep and eating right than you are with any combination of these chemicals.

Afterword - Intrinsic Motivation - Why We Do What We Do

As mentioned before, no one is productive 24/7. What helps keep us going though is an intrinsic motivation - motivation that comes from intangible internal factors. We write because we want to create art, not because we want to reap huge cash rewards. We create a business to solve a problem, not because we want to be on the cover of Forbes magazine. Think of your hobbies or passions, those are prime examples of intrinsic motivation. We all have that one friend who is obsessed with, and derives so much pleasure from an activity that we really have no interest in. That is the kind of motivation you must approach your work with, because if it is truly rewarding and something you truly desire, that motivation will keep you going through the tough periods.

When you find yourself procrastinating, take a step back and ask yourself - why am I doing this task? Remember to think of the bigger picture at hand and why you wanted to undertake the project in the first place. It is these moments that shape us and allow us to complete what is necessary to achieve our ultimate goals.

© Copyright 2017 James Oliver. All Rights Reserved.

Bibliography

[i] https://www.amazon.com/gp/product/1936891379/ref=as_li_tl?ie=UTF8&camp=1789&creative=9325&creativeASIN=1936891379&linkCode=as2&tag=jcpublishing-20&linkId=19803821da9aae1df17c97e85b48e897

[ii] Pychyl, T. A., Lee, J. M., Thibodeau, R., & Blunt, A. (2000). Five days of emotion: An experience sampling study of undergraduate student procrastination (special issue). Journal of Social Behavior and Personality, 15, 239-254.

[iii] http://www.rand.org/pubs/research_reports/RR1791.html

[iv] http://faculty.haas.berkeley.edu/brchen/2001-104.pdf

[v] **http://www.bentley.edu/newsroom/latest-headlines/mind-of-millennial**

[vi] http://www.apa.org/research/action/multitask.aspx

[vii] https://www.amazon.com/gp/product/1591846072/ref=as_li_tl?ie=UTF8&camp=1789&creative=9325&creativeASIN=1591846072&linkCode=as2&tag=jcpublishing-20&linkId=e0340d8bdb791844b1435e5e85cffa2d

[viii] https://www.youtube.com/watch?v=NHopJHSlVo4&vl=en

www.ingramcontent.com/pod-product-compliance
Lightning Source LLC
Chambersburg PA
CBHW030534220526
45463CB00007B/2824